LET'S VISIT INDIA

Let's visit INDIA

JOHN C. CALDWELL

BURKE

First published in Great Britain July 1965
Reprinted February 1967
Second edition April 1968
Third edition June 1974
Fourth revised edition November 1978
Fifth revised edition 1983
© John C. Caldwell 1960
New material included in this edition © Burke Publishing Company Limited 1965, 1969,
1974, 1978 and 1983.

ACKNOWLEDGEMENTS

The Publishers thank the following for permission to reproduce the illustrations in this book:
Douglas Dickins; The Government of India; I.C.A.; Monitor Press Features; Torge; U.S.I.S.
The cover photograph of the Taj Mahal is by Frederika Davis and was supplied by
Barnaby's Picture Library.
Thanks are also due to Garry Lyle for assistance in preparing this edition.

CIP data
Caldwell, John C.
    Let's visit India. – 5th ed. – (Let's visit)
    1. India – Social life and customs – Juvenile literature
    I. Title   II. Lyle, Garry
    954   DS421
    ISBN 0 222 00914 4   M O   9203760

Burke Publishing Company Limited
Pegasus House, 116-120 Golden Lane, London EC1Y 0TL, England.
Burke Publishing (Canada) Limited
Toronto, Ontario, Canada.
Burke Publishing Company Inc.
540 Barnum Avenue, Bridgeport, Connecticut 06608, USA.
Printed in Singapore by Tien Wah Press (Pte) Ltd.

Contents

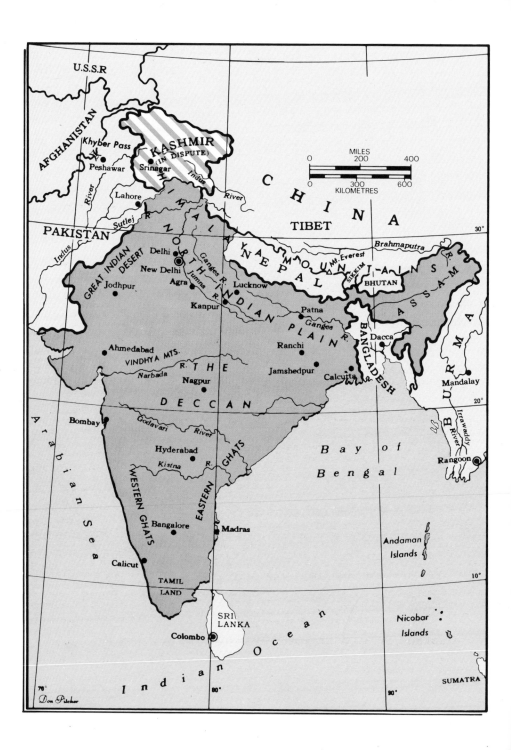

Let's Visit India

People often think of India as a strange and exotic country. The Indians, too, are thought to be "different" and to have peculiar customs which are difficult to understand. The sacred cow and the caste system, for example, are found only in India. But these differences are only a small part of the story. To know about India, we have to learn something of the living conditions of the Indian people and to try to understand their history and their hopes for the future. India is one of the oldest civilisations of the world. The forces which were active in her past are still there today and they have to be taken into account when we think of present-day India.

India is a huge and important country. The total population is in the region of 700,000,000 people. India has had great influence upon other countries in Asia. Indian culture and ideas have spread to every country in the East. It is interesting that Indian religions, Hinduism and Buddhism, were taken to other nations without war or conquest; they moved abroad peacefully.

During recent years, India has become important for another reason. Since the end of the Second World War, the world has been divided. There are the communist nations, led by Russia, and there are the Western nations, led by the United States. Sometimes, as in Korea, the trouble between them has led to bitter fighting.

The United States and its allies believe that nations can remain free of communist control by joining together in military alliances. The government of India has refused to join either side and has become the leader of the *neutralist* nations. These are countries that believe it is possible to have the friendship of both Communist nations and Western nations. They are all in Asia and Africa, and have followed India's leadership.

Being a member of the Commonwealth, India has close links with the United Kingdom and with the other Commonwealth nations. In spite of their different approach to world problems, they have maintained very friendly relations.

India is as interesting as it is important. It is a land of contrasts. Among its people are some of the richest men in the

One of the many ancient temples in India

world, but millions are among the poorest, and more of them are always hungry than in any other country.

A large part of the population of India cannot read or write, but India has produced some of the world's greatest literature—and also the longest poem ever written. It has 700,000 words.

Millions of Indians live almost exactly as did their forefathers centuries ago. There are also big modern cities. India is a land of towering snow-capped mountains; it is also a land of jungles, deserts, and terrible heat. The wettest spot in the world is in India, and there are also areas that have almost no rainfall.

Here is another unusual fact about India, one which shows us that India has unusual problems to solve. There are fifteen major languages and over 800 different dialects. No one

9

language is spoken by more than half the people. Because of this, English is still an associate official language in India, although Hindi is the official language.

Now let's learn more about India, its geography and climate, its people and their long history.

Carrying water from the village well

The Land and the People

From the map on page 6, you will see that India is shaped like a triangle with the point, or apex, in the south. Or we can compare its shape to that of a big ice-cream cone. The broad top of the cone is cold and white with the snow of the world's highest mountains. These are the Himalayas. In these same mountains is the highest peak in the world, Mt. Everest, over 29,000 feet (8,845 metres) high, which lies outside India, on the boundary between Tibet and Nepal.

The mountains descend into jungle-covered hills, and the hills descend to the great North Indian Plain. This is the second of India's four main geographical regions. It extends from the Bay of Bengal in the east to the Arabian Sea in the west. This part of India is sometimes called Hindustan. It is the centre of Indian culture and the part where most of the great cities are located. One language spoken here, Hindi, is the most important language of India.

India's most important rivers flow through the North Indian Plain. They are the Ganges—with its main tributaries the the Jumna and Gogra—and the Brahmaputra. From their sources in the Himalaya Mountains the Ganges and the

11

The Himalayas, the world's highest mountains

Brahmaputra flow for great distances through India and then into Bangladesh, India's eastern neighbour.

The long River Indus is also very important to India but this river does not flow through India itself. It rises in the mountains of Tibet and then flows through the disputed territory of Kashmir into India's western neighbour, Pakistan. However, some of its tributaries are partly in India and India uses their water to irrigate much of the North Indian Plain.

The southern reaches of the North Indian Plain extend to the Vindhya Mountains. Southward again, another range slopes down to a great plateau—an area of land which is fairly flat, but well above sea-level. This plateau is called the Deccan. It stands at an average height of about 2,000 feet (610 metres) above the sea, and is the third of India's four main regions. To the east and the west, rugged mountain ranges separate the Deccan from the sea. These are called *ghats*, meaning elevated

12

places. The Western Ghats are in south-west India, between the Deccan and the Arabian Sea. The Eastern Ghats, not as rugged nor as high, lie between the Deccan and the Bay of Bengal.

Between the Ghats and the sea, there is the coastal plain of southern India, the fourth major geographical area. This flat area along the Arabian Sea and the Bay of Bengal broadens out in the south, to become what is sometimes called Tamil Land because the Indians who live there are called Tamils. The flat plains of Tamil Land extend to the very tip of the cone and continue to a point at Cape Comorin. To the south lies the big island of Sri Lanka, separated from India by seventy miles (over 112 kilometres) of island-dotted ocean. The western shore of India is called the Malabar Coast; the eastern side is the Coromandel Coast.

The climates of India's four regions differ greatly. In the

Typical farm area

northern mountain and hill country it is cold in the winter, and temperate in the summer. In the North Indian Plain, summers are hot, and there are summer rains. Sometimes there are dust storms. The winters are mild, but sometimes at night it is quite cold. The Deccan is dry except during the *monsoon,* the period from June to September when the rainy season comes. Along the coast, especially in the coastal plains, the rainfall is very heavy, decreasing with the distance inland. There are parts of India, especially in the west and north-west where annual rainfall is less than eight inches (200 milli-metres). This means that the land there is always very dry much like the deserts of North Africa. Even in the Deccan there is so little rainfall, except during the monsoons, that the rivers often run dry. Along the south-east coast of India and in Assam, in the north-east, rainfall may total 400 inches (ten metres) a year.

About one-quarter of India is covered with trees. In the

A camel market in one of the desert areas of India

A view of the Himalayan foothills from Simla

mountainous and hilly areas, there are great expanses of forest and jungle. There are also jungles in the Western and Eastern Ghats, and in areas along the south-east and south-west coasts. India's area is about one-third that of the United States of America. Yet India has over three times as many people as the United States.

India is a mixture of peoples. In the south there are the very dark-skinned people known as the Dravidians. In the extreme east and along the northern borders there are hill people who are related to the races of Burma and Tibet. Living in the jungles of the south and west of India are 25 million people of many tribes: some of them are of mixed Malay and Mongolian descent. Then, throughout the plain of northern India there are people of Indo-European descent —descendants of the Aryans. We will read later how these Aryans came to India many centuries ago. In the mountain valleys of the north-west there are people who are blond, or

15

A father-and-son snake-charming team

partially blond, in contrast with the normal colouring associated with Indians.

Indians call their country *Bharat*. The name India comes from *Sindhu*, the Indian name for the Indus River. From Sindhu come the words Hind, Hindu (man of Hind), Hindustan, Ind and India.

In a country with so much variety in geography and climate and with so many different peoples, there are many different ways of life. But before we learn about these differences, let's learn something about some of India's neighbours.

In the north, India borders on China and Tibet, which is controlled by China. Along the northern border we also find two small countries, Nepal and Bhutan, mountainous and wild, and inhabited by many different tribes. These are independent nations with close relationships with India.

Nepal can now be reached quite easily by road or by plane. It is an interesting country for several reasons. Its mountain people, known as the Gurkhas, are among the best fighters in the world. For many years Gurkhas have fought in the British army and there are many Gurkha troops in the modern Indian Army. Nepal also is the home of the Sherpas, specially trained mountain climbers who are important members of every mountain-climbing expedition in the Himalayas. With their help, Sir Edmund Hillary conquered Mt. Everest, and Sherpas have helped many European expeditions climb other high mountains in the Himalayas.

Now let's look at the map once again. In the far north-

Women of Nepal

west, a corner of India extends to the Kunlun Mountains of China. This north-western section is called Kashmir, a beautiful area of waterways, mountains and lovely valleys. It is also an area of trouble and dispute, for although Kashmir is claimed and partly occupied by India, it has also been claimed and partly occupied by Pakistan. This is only one of the arguments between these two neighbouring countries which until recently were one country. We will learn more about these problems later.

If you look at the map again, you will see that in the east, India really has two different borders. There is a long border with Bangladesh, then a narrow corridor of Indian territory separating Nepal, Tibet, and Bhutan from Bangladesh. This corridor broadens out into a large area of India known as Assam, which joins with Burma to the east and with China to the north. Thus the eastern part of India is almost cut off from the rest of the country. It can be reached only by the narrow corridor that separates Bangladesh from Nepal and Bhutan. It looks as though the borders have been drawn to makes things difficult. In fact, there is no place in the world where the borders seem to make less sense than those between India and her neighbours.

From 1947 until 1970, India was bordered by Pakistan on the east and on the west, but then, after much bloodshed East

A man from Mysore

Village life is often simple. Many of its features—such as this water-jar—are the traditional ones which have been known in India through the ages

Pakistan became the independent state of Bangladesh. It is important for us to know why this happened, and why there were two halves to Pakistan, separated by nearly 1,000 miles (1,609 kilometres) of India. So instead of beginning our visit with an account of India's history long ago, we will start with the period when the countries that are now India, Pakistan and Bangladesh were one country governed by Britain. Then we shall ask how it was possible for Britain to control so large an area with so many people for so many years. The answer goes back into the ancient history of the Indian subcontinent and particularly to the religions that were followed by its people.

India as a British Colony

In September, 1499, Vasco da Gama arrived back in Portugal after a voyage of many months during which his fleet had visited Calicut, on the Malabar Coast of India. The cargo which da Gama had picked up in Calicut excited the people of Europe, and was to change the way of life of millions of people in Asia.

Vasco da Gama's magic cargo was spices—pepper, nutmeg, cloves. For the most part, the spices were not grown in India, for Calicut was at that time a great trading centre for Arab and Indian merchants who imported spices from the Molucca Islands, a part of modern Indonesia. These islands became known to Europeans as the Spice Islands.

At first, the trade in spices was much the most important reason for European interest in the East. Wars were fought because of pepper and other spices. The New World was actually discovered when explorers were travelling in search of these spices! Later, however, they lost some of their importance as trade in other goods—such as cloth and precious minerals—began to grow. When European countries took control of India and large parts of South-east Asia, they did it to protect and extend their own profitable trading activities.

Since early times, there had been some trade between Asia and Europe; but the two continents were separated by deserts and mountains, and by the powerful Ottoman Empire which was Moslem in religion and not on friendly terms with Christian Europe. It was not until the seafaring people of Western Europe built larger ships and dared to believe that the world was not flat that they began to explore far and wide. Even so, the journey from Europe to India and South-east Asia was long and dangerous. Ships sailed down the coast of Africa, around the Cape of Good Hope and into the Indian Ocean. The round trip might require several years; often ships disappeared and were never heard of again.

The early Portuguese explorers found other exciting products in the East including beautiful fabrics and gems. But it was the pepper and other spices that had most to do with exploring Asia. Europeans, most of whom were used only to salt and vinegar, were excited at what spice could do to make food more palatable.

Within a few years after Vasco da Gama visited India, many Portuguese ships were sailing into the Indian Ocean. These ships were large and well armed, and the resistance of the Arabs who controlled the Indian Ocean was quickly overcome. Soon a famous Portuguese sea captain, Alphonso de Albuquerque, established the first European settlement at Goa on India's west coast in 1505.

For almost a century Portugal controlled the spice trade, and a number of Portuguese trading posts were established in India, in Malaya and in the Spice Islands. But the Dutch, who were expert seamen and shrewd merchants, wasted no time in challenging Portugal's monopoly. Many Dutch ex-

India is now a land of great changes, where people are learning new ways. These Delhi schoolgirls, for example, study as hard as their brothers although at one time Indian girls did not attend school

peditions sailed round Africa and into the Indian Ocean so that by the year 1600 there were several Dutch trading posts in India. The Dutch eventually pushed the Portuguese out of the spice trade. Portugal now has nothing of the great area it once controlled. Its last colony—Goa—was occupied by India in 1961.

Soon after the Dutch gained control of the spice trade, they raised the price of pepper. Having a monopoly in the pepper trade meant that they could set any price they wished. In 1587, English merchants had been very much excited when Sir Francis Drake captured a Portuguese ship filled with spices. The cargo was sold for a fabulous sum in England!

So it was that English merchants decided to form a company to trade in spices, and in 1600 the British East India Company was established. Soon company expeditions were sailing to India and the Spice Islands, but they found the

23

Resting under the trees near an old town gateway

Dutch well established, and for some years Dutch and English ships were fierce rivals for the spice trade. In fact, the Dutch control of the Spice Islands made it so difficult to establish trading posts that the British turned to the mainland of Asia, to see what resources they might find there.

For a number of years, the British were too busy fighting the Portuguese to establish many trading posts. Then at last the Portuguese navy was defeated—in 1612 and again in 1614—and the Dutch became too involved in their affairs in the islands of Indonesia to compete with the British in India.

The first British settlement, called St. George, was established in 1639. This tiny fort was to become one of India's greatest ports, and is now called Madras. In 1661, the British also gained control of Bombay, on India's west coast. Bombay is now India's second largest city and a great seaport. In 1690, a trading-post was established at Calcutta on the Hooghly River. Calcutta was then only a village; it is now a city of 7,000,000 people, the largest in India.

The history of Europeans in India follows the pattern of their rivalry across the world. England and Holland carried their battles on the mainland of Europe to both America and the East. England prevailed in America and India, while the Dutch established themselves in Indonesia. But other powers, who were less successful, had to be content with much less influential and powerful positions in the East; Portugal was one of these.

India then had its own powerful rulers—the Moguls, descended from Turks who had invaded the country in 1525 and gradually taken control of it. But they began to lose power after 1707 when the Mogul emperor Aurangzeb died. His successors allowed the country to become divided into many independent kingdoms, some of them large, others very small. This lack of unity weakened India, and the British East India Company began to gain control. Between 1746 and 1761, its army defeated several Indian armies and also the French, who had become quite powerful in India. They had established trading centres, and were trying to drive the British out. Even when this French threat was over, the British had many more years of resistance from Indians before they gained control of almost all of what is now India, Pakistan and Bangladesh. From 1814 until 1818, they fought the Gurkhas in northern India. In 1840, they also subdued the people known as Sikhs who, like the Ghurkhas, are fierce Indian warriors.

But although much fighting took place the British often preferred to make arrangements with the rulers of the many independent Indian states, rather than to fight them. The heads of these states, rajahs and sultans, were allowed to keep much of their power in return for favours they granted to the British.

After the Sikhs were defeated, all India came under the rule of the East India Company. It is important to know that it was a business company, rather than the British government, which conquered and began to rule India. The East India Company had become so powerful that in 1852 it also conquered a valuable part of Burma. We might say that the company was a partner of the British government, but the

An old Mogul tomb in Delhi

soldiers in this partnership were paid by the company rather than by the Crown.

Unfortunately, there were some unscrupulous and self-seeking men in the East India Company, and many of its officials made great fortunes. People in England soon began to feel that the East India Company had too much power. Finally, Warren Hastings, one of the early governors, was brought to trial in England. The British government tried without success to impeach Hastings for dishonesties in India.

In time, the company lost its power and influence. The government of India became more truly a colonial government whose important decisions were made in London. The Governors-General sent from England did many things to create better government in India.

Several social reforms were carried out by the British and some of the cruel customs of Indian society were abolished. One such custom was *suttee* by which it was decreed that a widow must burn herself on the funeral pyre when her husband's body was cremated. There was also a custom which required the drowning of unwanted girl babies. In addition, at that time, slavery still existed in some parts of India. As well as doing away with these customs, the British rulers built new roads and harbours, and several railways. They also established a telegraph system and built schools and colleges which offered an English-style education in India.

Along with these reforms, there was some talk of eventually giving India her independence. The British thought that

A Hindu temple near Calcutta

their rule would prepare the Indians for self-government. Thomas Babington Macaulay, the brilliant nineteenth-century scholar and historian once said, "Whenever it comes, it will be the proudest day in British history." The day he was speaking of was the day when India became independent.

Yet, for more than a hundred years after Macaulay's declaration, India was to remain subject to Britain. This was the cause of much strife for, while India had welcomed the British as traders, it resented their staying on as rulers. In 1857, Indian resentment led to widespread revolt. The immediate result of this was a mutiny among Indian soldiers who had joined the British army. This mutiny, often called "The Indian Mutiny", soon spread far beyond the army. Much of northern India was in revolt for over a year and many cruel and bloody battles were fought. The Indian forces were led by those princes and rulers who had lost their kingdoms to the British and wanted to win them back. But they failed in their attempts and, by 1858, the British were more strongly established in India than ever before.

The Mutiny marks a very important stage in the story of India. Until it happened the British had governed through the East India Company. But the revolt convinced them that India needed a different form of government. Responsibility for the government of India was taken over by the British Crown in 1858. India became a British colony—the largest and most splendid of Britain's imperial possessions.

Another important effect of the revolt was that, with their

A school which was established by the British and is still run on British public school lines

defeat, the Indian princes lost all their power. The next challenge to British rule was to come from very different people. These were the people who wished to set up a modern and free society in India. Unlike the princes, they had no wish to revert to ancient ways.

There was no strong call for an end to British rule for more than a generation. This, meanwhile, was the heyday of the British in India. They were the most prosperous and scientifically advanced people in the world. They brought to India many of their finest talents—for India was the "jewel in the Empire's crown". The British gave India a strong and stable administration. Commerce and trade were extended and the country benefited in a thousand ways. In 1877, Queen Victoria was declared "Empress of India". Her subjects thought it their right and responsibility to govern the so-called "backward peoples".

It became fashionable for the sons of fine British families to spend some time in the India Service, or in the British army in India. Many British people spent their whole lives in India. Sometimes life was luxurious for them. Servants were readily available for domestic chores and, in the hot weather, British wives went to the "hill stations" which were summer resorts in the Himalayan foothills. These are still very popular.

British rule did much for India. Roads and railways were built. Among the great cities that were established is New Delhi, built next to old Delhi, the capital city of the Mogul Empire. The British brought peace and a settled administration to large parts of India which had suffered years of

A view of Simla, one of the British hill stations

A British-built canal. By building dams and canals the British brought water to many dry parts of India

turmoil. Uniform law was established and many cruel customs were abolished.

But though British rule brought many benefits to India, it was largely for the greater advantage of Britain herself. Indians soon came to demand a greater share in the running of their country. We shall read more of their fight for independence in a later chapter.

Now let's learn about India's ancient history and about the numerous conquerors who came into the North Indian Plain. These conquerors brought different religions with them, and in time religion became a great divider of the people. But India's long history is still glorious, and is filled with romance, fascination and accomplishment.

The First Invaders

Archaeologists are scientists who study the life and activities of ancient peoples. Often they try to answer the questions, "Who lived here first, and when? How did they live?" In 1921, archaeologists discovered the remains of a mysterious civilization in the valley of the Indus River. The Indus is the big river which flows from the mountains on India's northwest frontier through present-day Pakistan and into the Arabian Sea.

The Indus Valley peoples built big and well-planned cities almost 5,000 years ago. But these ancient cities are in the part of the Indus Valley which now is in modern Pakistan, so we will consider them as being the earliest known peoples who lived in Pakistan. Who then were the first peoples of India?

We have learned that there are many different peoples living in India, representing four of the five major branches of the human family. Thousands of years ago the most numerous people in India were probably the dark-skinned Dravidians. We do not know very much about the life of the Dravidians. As a matter of fact, the important period of India's past began when invaders came to push the Dravidians from the North Indian Plain.

About 2000 B.C. the first of many invaders pushed through the mountain passes from Central Asia. These people were vigorous nomads. They were fair-skinned and related to the ancient Greeks and Persians. We call these first invaders Indo-Aryans. They pushed into present-day Pakistan and into the North Indian Plain. The Dravidian people, who were no match for them, retreated steadily into southern India.

The invasions from Central Asia continued for over a thousand years until the newcomers had spread throughout the North Indian Plain from the Arabian Sea to the valley of the Ganges River. They built cities, and began to trade throughout the Indian peninsula.

Our knowledge of this long period of conquest and settlement comes from the ancient scriptural books called Vedas. The word *veda* means wisdom. For centuries before they were written down, the accounts of Aryan conquest passed from generation to generation by word of mouth. There are four Vedas which tell us the story of these long-ago days in India, much as the Bible tells us the ancient history of the Jewish people.

But there were more invaders to come before the Indo-Aryan people established themselves firmly in India. Six hundred years before Christ, Persian armies conquered much of India. In the fourth century, Alexander the Great also invaded India and conquered its northern parts. After his death in 323 B.C. one of his generals ruled this area. Then a young warrior named Chandragupta Maurya drove the Greeks from India and established a great Indian empire. We call this the Maurya Dynasty.

Seventh-century rock-carving in Madras

A grandson of the dynasty's founder, Asoka, became the most famous ruler of this period. The flag of modern India includes the many-spoked "wheel of Asoka". Asoka was a great warrior during the early years of his reign, but he came to hate bloodshed, and even discontinued the royal hunts and forbade the killing of animals for the royal table.

Asoka, who was a Buddhist, built many memorials to Buddhist saints. These were called stupas. One of Asoka's capital cities was located at Sarnath, and huge stone pillars fifty feet (over fifteen metres) high still remain from this period, over 2,200 years.

35

In 232 B.C., Asoka died, and soon the Maurya Empire began to fall apart. New invasions came from Central Asia, including tribes known as the Scythians and the Kushans. For over a thousand years after this, India's history was one of wars, invasions, and the rise and fall of small kingdoms.

There was a short period, from A.D. 320 to A.D. 480, when the Gupta Emperors united all of northern India. Under the Guptas, India was properous and peaceful. A great university was established, and it attracted students from all over Asia. It was during the Gupta Dynasty that the so-called Arabic system of numbering, which we use today, was invented. Hindu mathematicians developed the system of numbering from 1, 2, 3 to 10. The Persians borrowed the system from the Hindus, and the Arabs borrowed it from the Persians. The last borrower seems to have gained the most credit, for today we call this the Arabic system of numbering!

This camel is raising water by means of a "Persian Wheel", an ancient method still in use in modern India

The age of the Guptas is known as the Golden Age of Indian art and architecture. During this period the country was properous and much labour was used to build splendid monuments. The sculpture of the time reached a new level of excellence. Much progress was also made in the sciences and Indian medicine won fame in many lands. India had developed a highly civilised society. The prosperity of the country derived mainly from the produce of the fertile plains of northern India. Unfortunately, it always tempted invaders from the harsher lands to the north and west.

The Gupta Empire lasted less than two hundred years before it collapsed when new invaders called Huns came into India. Again the country experienced what had happened throughout its history. There were many small kingdoms, some lasting for years, others for only a short period.

Unlike China, India had few lengthy periods of strength and greatness. We have not space to mention all the dynasties and kingdoms, some of which existed among the Dravidian and Tamil peoples in the south.

The last of the long line of invaders were the Muslims who came to India during the Middle Ages. We shall learn more about them and their impact on India in a later chapter. The last invasion of all was to come from the sea—these invaders were the Europeans about whom we have already read.

However, in spite of many conquerors and long periods of war, the Indian way of life developed during these centuries.

This way of life and its religion have been very important, and we must learn something about them in order to understand more about India.

We have used the word Hindu in describing the Gupta mathematicians who invented the system of numbering we use to this day. Now let's learn what Hindu and Hinduism mean, and what effect Hinduism has had on India.

The Aryan invaders who poured into the North Indian Plain over the centuries developed a written language called Sanskrit which is the basis for most of India's modern languages. In time, the sacred Vedas, or Books of Wisdom, were written down in Sanskrit. Other great poems and books were written, developing the ideas of Hinduism that have had such effect on Indian culture. The *Mahabharata* is the longest poem ever written, in 100,000 couplets and 700,000 words. Another great epic poem beloved of Indians is the *Ramayana*. This great Hindu literature telling the story of wars and wanderings also follows the growth of the religious beliefs and system of thought that we call Hinduism. What are the main beliefs of Hindus?

The Hindus believe in a supreme creator who is called Brahma. There are many other gods including Vishnu (the preserver) and Siva (the destroyer). Hindus believe that life is marred by evil, and that the main objective of living is to become free of this evil. The only way the human soul can escape evil is to be reborn again and again, so that the evil is refined out little by little as each life is lived. A person may

38

Ploughing in southern India, near Bangalore

be reborn many times before the highest and purest state is reached.

Hindu society is organised according to a caste system. This probably began when the Aryans conquered the dark-skinned Dravidians. The tall, fair-skinned Aryans looked down on the Dravidians who did not share their religion. As a result, the Dravidians were given a lower status. Gradually, however, a much more elaborate system was built up.

Caste divides all people into groups according to birth and occupation. At the top are *Brahmans,* the priestly class. This word comes from the word for the supreme god—Brahma.

Beneath them are hundreds of castes. All of them, including the Brahmans, fall into four main divisions. They are the *Kshatriyas,* or warriors; the *Vaisyas,* who were farmers and merchants; and the *Sudras,* who were the serfs. Beneath the four castes come the casteless people sometimes known as the Untouchables.

We can see from this that the original divisions of Hindu society according to the caste system were not unlike the classes which existed in medieval Europe.

As society became more complicated and people learned new skills, the castes began to divide into sub-castes. Originally, birth and occupation were the two factors which decided a man's caste. With the growth of new occupations, new factors assumed importance. For example, as gold jewellery gained popularity, a caste of goldsmiths grew up. Similarly, the bakers, confectioners and money-lenders, and

40

An Indian village

people in countless other trades, each had their own groupings.

Up to a point, the caste system was nothing more than a way of dividing labour among the community, like the guilds of Europe. But after a while the caste rules became more rigid. A person could marry only within his caste. He could only have social relations with members of his own caste. In addition, rules were laid down for eating and drinking. A man could not accept food from a member of a lower caste. Worst of all, the so-called Untouchables led a painful life for they were denied all common privileges.

Modern India has done much to correct the evils of the caste system as they finally developed. The idea of untouchability is now forbidden by law. Those people who suffered from it in the past are now given special privileges in compensation. Much of the good work is the result of the efforts of Mahatma Gandhi, the great Indian leader of modern times, for he always fought for the unprivileged. Even so, much remains to be done before the evils of the system are finally removed.

41

The caste system is only a part of Hinduism. This religion is distinguished by the depth and splendour of its thought. The *Vedas,* or ancient Aryan hymns, are among the most significant religious texts of the world. The *Gita* is the most beloved of religious books among the Hindus. It has fascinated scholars and ordinary people in many parts of the world.

The Vedas say that the cow is sacred, and a good Hindu cannot kill one. There are nearly 200,000,000 cattle in India, or about thirty cows to every hundred people, and cows wander about everywhere, even in the biggest cities.

Among other important religious groups are India's ten million Sikhs. The Sikh religion was founded by Guru (which means Great Teacher) Nanak in the fifteenth century. Sikhs are not divided into castes and they worship one god rather than many gods. A Sikh man will never cut his hair or his beard. The hair is tied up under a beautiful turban, and the beard is sometimes skilfully braided. All Sikh men wear a special bracelet on the wrist, much as Catholics wear little crosses, and they carry a small knife. In olden days Sikhs wore swords rather than small knives, for they were famous fighters. They once led a revolt against the British; but after their defeat, many joined the British army where they distinguished themselves by their warlike qualities. Today this warrior sect provides a large number of the troops of the Indian army. They are also skilled and hard-working farmers in their native province of Punjab.

Jainism is another Indian religion that developed from

42

A Sikh worshipper standing in front of the Golden Temple at Amritsar

Hinduism. It was established about 600 B.C. by Mahavira Jnatiputra. Jains have even more respect for the lives of animals than do other Hindus. They will not kill any living thing, and do not believe in violence of any kind. As we shall learn later, the Jain idea of Ahimsa, or preservation of life, was used in India's struggle for independence from British rule.

There are about 100,000 followers of the Parsi (or Parsee) religion in India. Fire is sacred to the Parsi whose religion was founded by Zoroaster in Persia about 1000 B.C. A Parsi, because of his worship of fire, will not smoke or pour water on fire. A Parsi must bathe before he prays, and he must pray every morning and every night. When a Parsi dies, the body is placed within what is called a Tower of Silence, and left

43

to be picked clean by vultures, which are large flesh-eating birds. Most Hindus are cremated after death, but this would be a misuse of fire for a Parsi. The Parsi community is small in numbers because no one may become a convert; only a descendent of a Parsi may be a Parsi. But Parsis became important to India because they quickly accepted Western ways. They became teachers, scientists, and excellent businessmen. India's greatest modern steel company was founded by and is operated by a Parsi.

There are about fifteen million Christians in India, making Christianity India's third largest religion. According to legend, St. Thomas journeyed to the Malabar Coast, and as a result of his preaching, a thriving Christian community developed in the second century. These people, living in the state of Kerala, call their church the Syrian Christian Church. Many Indians were converted after the Europeans came to India. The influence of both Portugal and England resulted in the growth of the Christian community in the country.

Now we come to another great religion, established in

Pumping water for rice fields; another ancient method

India, but with few present-day Indian followers. About the same time as the Jain religion was founded, there were numerous Indians who were opposed to the caste system, and especially to the power of the Brahmans. They were also critical of the power of the many priests and of the complicated ceremonies of the Hindu religion. Among those opposed to these things was a man named Gautama Siddhartha who came to be called the *Buddha,* or Enlightened One.

Although he was born a nobleman, Buddha was opposed to caste, although he believed in reincarnation or man's rebirth. He also believed that life was evil but that one escaped this evil by good deeds, pure thoughts, and by giving up worldly desires. The emphasis was on a conscious effort by each individual to avoid all violence contributing to the sum of evil in the world.

Buddha lived for eighty years, and gave up his own life to preach his beliefs, wandering through India as a humble monk. We have already read that the Emperor Asoka became a Buddhist. At one time Buddhism was the leading religion of India. Although there are now only four million Buddhists in India, Buddhism has become the religion of over 500 million people elsewhere in Asia.

This is a good time for us to realize how much influence India has had on the rest of Asia. Even before Buddhism crossed into China, some Indians were taking either Buddha's message or Hinduism and its sacred books, together with the Sanskrit language, to South-east Asia. Nearly 2,000 years

A Rajput veteran. The Rajputs are members of the soldier caste and claim descent from the Kshatriyas

ago, Indian colonists were sailing across the ocean to the Malay Peninsula, to Indochina, and to the islands of Indonesia. India's lasting influence on these countries of Asia has been mainly cultural. Long after the original colonists were absorbed into their new countries, or had returned to India, their customs and religion prevailed.

Sons of the Prophet

In the year A.D. 711, Arabs had begun to settle around the mouth of the Indus River in what is now Pakistan. These Arabs were followers of the Moslem (or Muslim) religion. They conquered territory in the valleys of the Indus, but for over two centuries they did not have much effect upon India.

Then in A.D. 998, a Moslem army led by the Amir Mahmud of Ghazni began to raid Indian territory from Afghanistan. The Hindus fought bravely against the new invaders, but they were no match for the Moslem warriors, who used swift Arab war horses against the slow Indian war elephants. There were many other reasons for the success of the invaders. One was that their opponents were divided among themselves and incapable of coming together. In addition, the caste system weakened them, for only one section of the population—the warrior class—were supposed to fight.

These new invaders brought with them a religion which became the greatest divider of all. In fact, it not only divided people, but in time created two independent nations. It was this religious division that led to the strange geographical partition of the Indian subcontinent when the British finally withdrew.

For many years, the Moslems continued to raid and occupy Indian territory. Finally in A.D. 1191, a powerful Moslem named Mohammed Ghori began to raid, and gradu-

The Rajput fortress of Amber near Jaipur. The Rajputs, a warrior caste, fought the Moslems for many years

ally occupied large parts of India. For the next five hundred years, most of the country was under Moslem rule, and in 1526 the Moslem Mogul Dynasty was founded, which became the most powerful in India's history.

The religion of India's new rulers was founded by Mohammed, who was born in Arabia in the sixth century A.D. Believers in this religion are also called Mohammedans, and the religion is sometimes known as Islam. The teachings of Mohammed the Prophet are written down in a sacred book called the Koran. These beliefs are totally different from the beliefs of Hindus. Moslems believe in one God, and they hold that all people are created equal. The idea of caste was so strange to the Moslems that they could not accept it, nor could they understand the Hindus having many gods.

Already divided into many small states, India was at first divided even further by the powerful new religion which gained many converts in the course of time. But soon the

Moslems began to rule as Indians rather than as foreign conquerors. The Mogul Emperor, Akbar the Great, went so far as to try to develop a new religion which would unite his subjects. Just as the Aryans had entered India as invaders, and then settled down as people of the country, so the Moslems, too, made India their home.

Unfortunately, their religion remained an obstacle to the unity of the people of India as a whole. Some Mogul rulers, unlike Akbar, treated Hindus badly. They were made to pay special taxes and were persecuted in many other ways. The result was that these religious and social differences persisted for centuries.

The Moguls were great builders as well as good fighters, and some of India's most famous buildings were erected by Mogul emperors, or shahs. The world-famous Taj Mahal at Agra is often called the most beautiful building on earth. It was built by the Shah Jahan as a memorial to his favourite wife when she died young.

The Taj Mahal, one of the world's most beautiful buildings

During the centuries of Moslem raids and rule, many more Moslems came into India, while many Indians became Moslems. The people living in the valley of the Indus River became Moslem in great numbers. This is the area closest to the mountain passes through which the Moslem invaders came. It is also close to the Arabian Peninsula from which other Moslems came by sea.

In some parts of India, there were not many converts to the new religion. However, in the extreme eastern part, around the mouth of the Ganges River, most of the people became Moslems. Altogether, by the time Great Britain gained control of the Indian subcontinent, about one out of every four people was a follower of Mohammed.

So great was the division caused by religion that, when the country finally gained independence, the Moslems demanded and obtained a separate State. This resulted in the curious boundaries of India and Pakistan, since it was the two areas which became East and West Pakistan which had the largest Moslem communities. There are, however, over sixty million Moslems in India. Today India is a State without an official religion. Her citizens include people of many different religions.

Although it existed in name for many years, the Mogul Empire began to fall apart in 1707. There were many revolts against the Moguls; and, as happened so frequently in India's history, numerous small independent kingdoms were established. There were independent Hindu states and indepen-

The principal mosque in Delhi

dent Moslem states so that India became more divided than ever. It was during this period after 1707 that the British East India Company began to gain control of India. By the middle of the nineteenth century, this control was complete.

Now that we have read about India's history and of the reasons why it was easy for Great Britain to control so populous a land, let's learn how independence was finally achieved.

Many countries of the world have won their freedom after years of hard military struggles. In sharp contrast, *no* armies, *no* generals were involved in India's fight for freedom. India's independence was achieved mainly by following non-violent methods, an adaptation of the ancient Jain idea of Ahimsa.

The Struggle for Independence

As we have seen, at the end of the period of Mogul rule, the country had been split up into a number of small states which were often hostile to each other. This made it possible for the British to gain a foothold in India and gradually extend their rule over the entire country. The Indians could not match the advances already made by Britain in the Industrial Revolution. Nevertheless, they had a constant desire, even at this time, to regain freedom. This took the form of the armed revolt of 1857 about which we read earlier.

Some time later, however, the call for independence was renewed in a fresh form. Instead of weapons, the new leaders were armed with ideas. As communications improved and as the effect of the English schools began to be felt, Indians came into contact with modern European thought. Their demand for greater privileges had its parallel in the advances made by the common people in the more powerful countries of Europe. Perhaps the most important reason for this was the spread of education in the English language. Many English schools were set up by missionaries, and often their pupils went on to study at universities established by the government.

A few Indians went to England to study. Educated Indians began urging their countrymen to learn about the rest of the world, to become educated and learn new ways. Indian leaders also began a Hindu revival. This means that they urged

There are cowboys in India too! These Indian boys are learning how
to breed and raise healthier cattle

their people to remember the glories of the past and to learn more about the accomplishments of their great kings so that they might gain a sense of national future.

In 1885, a number of educated Indians formed an organization called the Indian National Congress, which met at Poona, near Bombay. Only seventy people attended the first meeting, and of these only two were Moslems. The National Congress was not at first a political group. It met in a different city each year, and its leaders were mainly interested in social reform. Some members urged the British to start compulsory education; others were interested in projects to help the millions of Untouchables and other low-caste people.

However, each year there was more discussion of self-government, more criticism of British rule and more demand for change. Those leaders who wanted moderate reforms were ousted by others who called for complete independence. In 1907, the great Indian patriot Tilak thrilled his fellow-countrymen with the words: "*Swaraj* (self-government) is my birthright and I will have it." By the time the First World War began, in 1914, the leaders of the Indian National Congress were all echoing Tilak's cry.

We must understand that most of the Indian leaders had no hatred for the British. In the war, Indians fought alongside British troops. Nor did they wish to turn their backs on all that the British had achieved in India. They appreciated what progress had been made—but, of course, they were also very well aware of the obligations imposed upon them by foreign rule. Their united call was for total independence.

India's struggle for independence continued for many years, and among its leaders we have space to mention only three men. Mohandas Gandhi became the best known and India's greatest hero. The other two were father and son, Motilal and Jawaharlal Nehru. Motilal, the father was a wealthy lawyer who became one of Gandhi's most active supporters. Jawaharlal became India's first prime minister and one of the world's best-known statesmen.

Gandhi was born in 1869 near Bombay. He came from an orthodox Hindu family who observed their traditional religious customs. Because young Gandhi wanted to be a lawyer, he went to England to study. In his autobiography, he describes how he almost starved until he discovered a vegetarian restaurant! In 1891, Gandhi returned to India, and two years later he went to South Africa to take up legal practice.

Gandhi became a successful and prosperous lawyer. He also became interested in the problems of the many Indians living in South Africa. The Indians there suffered great discrimination from the European residents and from the government. The young lawyer took up his countrymen's fight for better working conditions, for more rights and for an end to discrimination.

We have read about Ahimsa, the idea of preservation of life or non-violence, advocated by the religious teacher who founded Jainism in the sixth century. Gandhi began to study

**The former British Viceroy's House lit for the festival
of Divali. The President of India now lives here**

and to use Ahimsa. Under his leadership, thousands of
Indians in South Africa simply sat down on their jobs or
went on hunger strikes. They accepted arrest and would
never fight back. The courage of the Indians aroused public
opinion in England and in India, and the South African
government eventually made many of the changes demanded
by Gandhi.

When Gandhi returned to India, after a visit to England,
he was a public hero. He became known as the Mahatma,
which means the Great Soul. It is interesting that on his visit
to England, which took place in 1914 just as England went to
war, Gandhi urged all Indians to support the British war
effort.

In India, Gandhi established an *ashram* or school, and
many Indians came to hear him teach. He believed that India
could win its freedom through Ahimsa, or as he said, "by sym-

56

pathy, patience, and long-suffering." Within a few years, Gandhi had an opportunity to try non-violence on a national scale.

In 1919, the British government passed a number of laws to help control terrorism in India. There had been cases of Indians bombing trains, or shooting British soldiers from ambush. The new laws, called the Rowlatt Acts, gave the government power to arrest and judge people without trial, or to put suspected terrorists in prison without trial. Indian leaders were opposed to these laws. They said that they were undemocratic and gave the government far too much power.

The British built roads like this one throughout India

Gandhi appealed to his countrymen to observe a *hartal,* or day of prayer, in opposition. Everyone was urged to stop work, to close shops and to fast.

Unfortunately, the non-violent approach of the Indians was not able to last out to the end. There were riots, soldiers were called in to restore order, and they fired into the crowds. Gandhi was arrested, and although he was released in a few days, the news of his arrest caused more riots.

In the city of Amritsar, the Sikh city near Lahore, the rioting became serious. A British general who arrived with some soldiers foolishly ordered his men to fire again and again into a great crowd of people. The people were merely listening to speeches, and the firing began without warning. Nearly 1,500 men, women and children were killed or injured.

The news of the Amritsar massacre spread and caused great agitation throughout the country. This was the turning-point of the independence movement. The Indians who had formerly not been involved in it were now shocked into the realisation that their foreign rulers must go.

In 1921, Mahatma Gandhi led a nation-wide non-co-operation movement. The Indians hoped that by not paying taxes or participating in the running of the country in any way, they would make it impossible for the government to function. Students left their schools and colleges, and all kinds of ordinary people prepared themselves to go to jail, if necessary, in defiance of British authority. India had never seen anything like this before. The whole country was united.

This unified effort was very successful but it was marred by an act of mob violence which pained Gandhi deeply. He decided that the country was not yet ready for the discipline of non-violence and he called the whole movement off. This was not a popular move, but Gandhi placed principle above all other considerations. For him, the means was as important as the end.

The British government was also shocked by the Amritsar massacre, by the bombings and murders by terrorists. The British were anxious to make changes and to give the people more voice in their government, but they were not prepared to give as much as the Indians demanded. Besides, differences arose among the Indians themselves. For several years, Moslem leaders co-operated with Hindus, and many joined the National Congress. Although there were 100 million Moslems in India, they were not well organized. Moslem leaders became afraid that self-government would leave them without protection from the more numerous and better-organized Hindus. These fears led to the formation of a Moslem political group called the Muslim League. Under the leadership of Mohammed Ali Jinnah, the Muslim League became better organized to fight for conditions that would assure them equality with Hindus.

Perhaps the biggest problem was that British reforms were too slow. The people, whether Moslem or Hindu, wanted independence at once and not in gradual steps. Gandhi began to turn against the British who had arrested and imprisoned him on several occasions. And he began to share leadership with Jawaharlal Nehru who had also been educated in England and had returned to India with many ideas about how to help his people.

In 1930 another movement of defiance took place. The government controlled the salt business and taxed all salt produced or sold. Gandhi selected the salt tax as a symbol of oppression. On March 12th, he began a march to the sea which was far away from his headquarters. When Gandhi and his followers reached the sea, they picked up pinches of natural salt that had dried out from the water. This was to symbolize defiance of the government and the salt tax.

Immediately a new civil disobedience campaign began. This time it was a great success, and the business life of India became paralyzed. Once again, Gandhi was arrested, and 60,000 other members of the Congress with him.

Then, on September 3, 1939, Great Britain declared war on Germany, and the Viceroy of India, representing the British Crown, proclaimed that India also was at war. The Congress Party protested on the grounds that the consent of the people had not been obtained, and Gandhi announced that as a believer in non-violence he could not support the war.

In 1941, the war took a new turn when Japan attacked Pearl Harbour and captured Malaya and Singapore. Japanese armies then occupied Burma, invaded eastern India and bombed Calcutta.

An old woman using the spinning wheel that Gandhi made a
national symbol of independence

These events divided the Congress. Gandhi wanted all British troops to leave India, and, as he said, "leave India in God's hands." Other leaders wanted to fight against Japan and argue about freedom later. Nehru was willing for India to help Great Britain but only if India were granted immediate independence.

The British could not afford to have trouble in India in the middle of a desperate war. The government sent Sir Stafford Cripps, a man who had long advocated independence for India, to work out a solution. After meeting with Moslem and Hindu leaders, Cripps offered India complete independence as a member of the British Commonwealth of Nations. He promised that all British troops would leave; and that the new India could, if it wished, leave the Commonwealth and become completely free. However, he said that these things could not be granted while Great Britain was in a life-and-death struggle with Japan and Germany. In other words, the Indians could have what they wished *after* the war was won.

Every major Indian political party, including the Muslim League, turned the offer down. Gandhi threatened to declare another nation-wide disobedience campaign. Quickly the British Government arrested him, along with Nehru and hundreds of other leaders.

After the end of the Second World War, Great Britain had a new government led by the Labour Party whose leaders had always urged Indian independence. The British people had suffered much during the war. They were tired of the squabbling in India. As far as most people in England were concerned, the sooner India was free the better. Therefore Great Britain offered India complete independence. The new nation would be a dominion within the British Commonwealth of Nations, or it could decide to cut all ties with England. A Constituent Assembly would be elected, and this body would be responsible for drafting a constitution.

But differences between Moslem and Hindu leaders had become so great that no constitution could be drafted or government established which would satisfy both groups.

On August 16th, 1946, the Moslem leaders called a *hartal,*

A scene in Kashmir

or day of prayer. They wanted to bring attention to their views on freedom. Terrible riots broke out between Moslems and Hindus. In Calcutta alone, over 5,000 people were killed. The Muslim League leaders can perhaps be blamed for this particular event. On the other hand, Congress leaders, including Nehru, had made statements which frightened the Moslems, who became certain that the Hindus would control the new government.

The idea of partition, or separate Moslem and Hindu countries, had been suggested from time to time. The British were opposed to this idea. The roads, postal and telegraph systems had been planned for one big country. There were some Hindus and some Moslems living in every province or state, and in every independent state. The big state of Kashmir was ruled by a Hindu maharajah, while most of the people were Moslem. Hyderabad was ruled by a Moslem, but the people were Hindus. But, in spite of these problems, division into two separate nations seemed to be the only solution.

We have already learned that most of the people living in the Indus Valley were Moslems, and that there were also many Moslems in eastern India. British, Moslem and Hindu leaders worked together to try to draw boundaries which would create Moslem states in the Indus Valley region and in the part of eastern India along the lower Ganges and Brahmaputra rivers. However, it was impossible not to draw boundaries that would leave millions of Moslems living in India and millions of Hindus living in either part of the proposed new Moslem state, to be called Pakistan. It was decided that the many independent princely states would decide later on whether to be a part of India or a part of Pakistan, or try to remain independent.

In England, the bill granting complete independence was introduced in Parliament on July 4th, 1947, and was quickly passed so that at midnight on August 14th, India and Pakistan became free and independent members of the British Commonwealth of Nations. But independence did not solve the Moslem-Hindu problem. It only became worse. Within a few days, riots broke out in many parts of the subcontinent. Moslems attacked Hindus, Hindus attacked Moslems; sometimes Sikhs killed both Moslems and Hindus. Hundreds of villages were burned, and tens of thousands of men, women and children were killed. Thousands of Hindus, finding themselves living in the new Moslem Pakistan, tried to escape. Moslems left living in Indian territory fled toward one of the two sections of Pakistan. Huge caravans, often numbering 50,000 people, travelled on foot, carrying everything they owned. Often the escaping caravans were attacked and burned, and the people murdered or kidnapped. By the end of the year, nearly twelve million people had fled their homes and hundreds of thousands of people had been killed.

For a time, it appeared that nothing could stop the killing of Hindus by Moslems, and of Moslems by Hindus. Then it was that Mahatma Gandhi won a great victory. He made an appeal for a nation-wide day of prayer and fasting. Moslems and Hindus alike came to their senses, and for a time there was peace.

However, peace between Hindus and Moslems did not last long. New trouble broke out over the State of Kashmir. Moslems were afraid that the Hindu maharajah would join India. An invasion by tribesmen from Moslem areas in Pakistan sought to settle the issue by removing the ruler by force. The tribesmen defeated the Kashmiri troops and advanced to within a short distance of the capital. The maharajah then joined his State to India and asked for help. This help was given. Indian troops were flown into Kashmir. They saved the capital and engaged in battle with the invaders who now included troops of the Pakistan army.

For a while, it appeared that India and Pakistan would go to war. There was a new wave of hatred in both countries.

A rural family typical of India's poverty-stricken millions

Once again, Gandhi appealed for reason. On January 13th, 1948, he started a fast. He hoped that by starving himself as an example of self-sacrifice, he could persuade other Hindus to overcome their hatred of Moslems. Two weeks later, Gandhi was murdered by a Hindu who believed him to be too soft with the Moslems.

Perhaps in death Gandhi won his greatest victory; for his murder shocked Moslems and Hindus alike, and made them ashamed. Men of both nations realized that they could not afford to begin killing one another again.

Mahatma Gandhi deserves much of the credit for India's independence. Sometimes his disobedience campaigns did not work; sometimes Ahimsa ended in fighting. But for years Gandhi was a symbol to his people.

But although Gandhi's death averted war between Hindus and Moslems, it did not solve all the problems between India and Pakistan. It did not alter the map of the new India, which was carved up so strangely. The boundaries between India and Pakistan are still based on religion rather than race or language, or natural borders such as rivers or mountains. We will read later about some of the problems caused by these boundaries. Now let's learn about modern India, its government, and how its people live.

India Today

Soon after becoming independent and separate from Pakistan, India drafted a constitution and set up a permanent government. Thus India became a republic; she is a member of the British Commonwealth of Nations but is *not* a dominion. This means that relations with Great Britain are not as close as they are in the case of Canada or Australia.

India has a parliament, made up of two houses in some ways like the two houses of the British parliament. The upper house is called the *Rajya Sabha* or Council of States, and has not more than 250 members. The lower house is called the *Lok Sabha* or House of the People. It has about 530 members. Parliament is the lawmaking body, and its members are elected by the people.

The President of India is elected for five-year terms by the members of Parliament and the members of state legislatures. The Vice President is elected by members of Parliament. The President is not the head of the government. He appoints a Prime Minister who, in turn, selects his cabinet—called the Council of Ministers. In this way, the government of India is very similar to that of the United Kingdom.

India is divided into twenty-two states and nine territories. The territories include some mountainous frontier areas, islands in the Bay of Bengal, and Delhi. New Delhi, the capital, is not a part of any state but is governed as a part of the Delhi Territory.

Each state has an elected legislature of one or two houses. Each state governor, however, is appointed by the President. This means that in India the central, or federal, government has more power than the state governments.

There are several political parties in India but for many years the Congress Party was more powerful than all the others. We have read about the Indian National Congress that first met in 1885. This organisation became the Congress Party and it won control of India's government immediately after independence. Jawaharlal Nehru became its parliamentary leader and India's first prime minister. He continued in this office until his death in 1964.

The next prime minister, Lal Bahadur Shastri, died after only two years in office. He was followed by Mrs. Indira Gandhi, the daughter of Nehru (and not related to Mahatma Gandhi). Under Mrs. Gandhi, the Congress Party grew even

India's flag. It has bands of saffron yellow, white and green, and includes a blue wheel of Asoka copied from a carved pillar at Sarnath

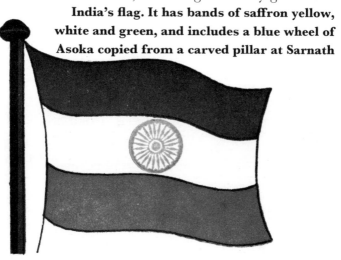

more powerful; for a time it could almost be said that India had a one-party government. However, Mrs. Gandhi and her party quickly lost their popularity when they began to act in a way which seemed undemocratic. In the elections of 1977 they were very heavily defeated by a group of parties called the Janata Coalition but the parties of the coalition soon found that they could not agree and their government collapsed.

Meanwhile, there had also been much disagreement among the members of the Congress Party. This led to the formation of a new party by Mrs. Gandhi's supporters. It is called the Indira Congress Party and has been the ruling party since it won a very large majority in the elections of 1980.

India's government is quite strong now, in spite of the many difficulties which the nation faced when it became independent. All of the hundreds of independent princely states had to decide whether to become a part of India or of Pakistan or to remain independent. None chose to be independent. The organization of India had to be changed as the princely states joined the nation. New boundaries were drawn. Before the present system of states and territories could be established, there were serious troubles. Most of these troubles were over language and state boundaries. Often there were bloody riots as people speaking the same language objected to new boundaries which did not include all people speaking that langauge.

India's first election took place in 1952. It was the largest election ever held in history, and took four months. At that time, 83 per cent of the people could not read. Each party and independent candidate was given a symbol so that illiterate people would know for whom they were voting. There were altogether 224,000 voting booths. In spite of these difficulties, a large proportion of people voted.

Language still remains one of India's problems. The Constitution made Hindi the official language. However, many of the best newspapers and magazines are published in English; English is the language of business, of the courts and also of parliament. It was also an official language of India until 1965; now it is called an associate language used for some government work and in many institutes of higher education. We will learn more about Hindi and the other important languages in the next section.

The Indian Constitution guarantees freedom of speech and of religion. It abolishes Untouchability. People may no longer be denied better jobs because of the caste into which they were born. However, the caste system which has existed for hundreds of years cannot be completely abolished overnight. Laws do not necessarily change people's ways of thinking about race or religion. Caste is still a problem in India.

Indians of different religions have made great progress in learning to live and work together. There are Sikhs, Hindus, and Moslems in high government positions. In spite of partition, there are over 60 million Moslems in India—more than live in any nation of the Moslem Middle East.

Now let's learn what life would be like if you lived in India. What are houses like, what food is eaten, what clothing is worn by the people of modern India?

There is no place in the world where one's daily life depends as much on religion as in India. If you lived in India, even your name might depend on your religion. If your last name were Singh, you almost certainly would be a Sikh. *All* Sikhs are named Singh; but not all people named Singh are Sikhs. If your last name were Khan, you would be from a Moslem family. Also, if you were a boy named Muhammed, Ali, Ahmad, or Husain, you would be a Moslem. Most names ending in "walla", such as Daruwalla, are Parsi. The last names Iyer or Iyengar are common, and always belong to southern Indian Brahman families.

If your family were high-caste Hindu, you would probably eat no meat at all, and no eggs. Lower-caste Hindus eat only mutton, no pork, and especially not beef. Moslems eat mutton, sometimes beef but never pork. Among educated modern Indians in the big cities, these dietary laws are not so important as they once were. There are Indians who eat meat and eggs, who use knives and forks, who live in every way much as we do. However, in this book we want to learn about *average* people. And among average Indians, living conditions, food, religious beliefs have not changed very much from the past.

We have been talking about food, so let's first learn about the daily food of an average Indian family. Notice the picture

A village near New Delhi with thatch-roofed houses

of an Indian man cooking. He is making *chapatties*, which look like pancakes; they are made from wheat and are baked into thin, unleavened cakes.

For most Indians, chapatties are an important part of every meal. They are eaten with curry, made with vegetables and meat. Sometimes, the curry spices have so much red chili pepper that it is terribly "hot" for a European, but many Indians like their curry to be much milder than Europeans imagine.

If you were to sit down to an Indian meal, you would probably sit on the floor. There would be no knives or forks on the low table placed before you. Indians eat with their

73

fingers, and chapatties are very helpful. Instead of having to dip your fingers into the curry stew, you would use pieces of chapatti to pick up each mouthful. Often a big banana leaf is used instead of a plate.

Food is somewhat different in the various parts of India. In southern India, rice is the most important cereal. In northern India, wheat made into chapatties is the most important. In some places, *jawar,* a kind of millet, is the basic food. Jawar is baked into cakes which are thicker and larger than chapatties, and are called *bhaker.* If your family were well-to-do, there would be more rice and less wheat and jawar in your daily food.

Making chapatties

A woman of the south
drawing water from
the village well

From the pictures in this section, you can see that most
Indians live simply. In some parts of India, houses are
rectangular and flat-topped. In other parts, the houses have
cone-shaped roofs made of thatch. Those in our picture look
much like houses we might expect to see in Africa. More of
these are seen in southern India.

The average low-income home has very little furniture,
and the floors are either of hard-packed mud or dried cow
dung. Many people still use simple implements passed down
through the centuries. On page 76 there is a strange picture.
The white stuff is home-made noodles. The noodles are hung

75

on the branches of a tree to dry. The woman's face is covered because she is in purdah—that is, she will not let her face be seen, except when she is inside her own home. Purdah is a Moslem custom now followed by many Hindu women. Moslems believe their women must be very modest, must never mix socially with men, must always keep their faces covered when they are outside the home.

The pictures will also give us an idea of Indian clothing. Since it is hot most of the year, clothing is light and loose.

A woman in purdah

Men wear a *dhoti*, a long piece of cotton cloth wrapped around the waist and with one piece passed between the legs. This gives the dhoti a gathered, baggy look. Many boys wear shorts and, in the hot months, nothing else. Of course, in the big cities many men wear Western-style clothing. Loosely wound turbans are worn by most men instead of hats. Even small boys have turbans. We have read about the fancy turbans worn by Sikhs. Turbans are made in all shades, pale or bright, and are very colourful.

The most popular dress for women is the *sari*, which may be very plain or, among wealthy people, very rich and beautiful. The sari is a very long wide piece of cloth which is first of all wound around the woman's waist, with some pleats in front. The remaining length of material is then drawn up across her shoulder or draped gracefully over her head. The exact method of draping a sari often differs according to the part of India from which a woman comes. A tight short-sleeved blouse and a floor-length petticoat are worn under the sari.

If you lived in India you might not go to school. Education is one of the country's biggest problems. Since independence, the government has built many schools, and free education is now available to all children. However, it is not easy for some children to take advantage of it. And it may be many years before all children can be educated. At present, about one-fifth of the children in India between the ages of six and eleven have no school education.

An open-air class in a village school

One of our pictures shows an Indian boy named Samsingh. He is on his way to school. In one hand he is carrying some books; in the other hand he has a lantern and a winnowing basket. Samsingh, like many other Indian boys, will go to school during the day; then he must work far into the night, helping a farmer with the rice harvest.

On the facing page there is a picture of a school in action. The Indian government will supply a teacher for any village which will provide a building. You can see that this school building is very crude, but at least the children can study here.

Indian boys and girls study arithmetic, science and history. They begin studying in their own langauge, but if they go very far in school, they must study English; for English is the chief medium of higher education.

Although the Indian Constitution recognizes fifteen different Indian languages, about 40 per cent of the people speak Hindi, which was developed from the Sanskrit of the Aryans who came to India centuries ago. It is strange that the other Sanskrit languages of northern and central India, although written in the same script, often sound quite different from each other when spoken. For instance, "Let's take a trip to India" would sound like this in Hindi: *Ham bharat ser kar aien.* But in Marathi, which is spoken in South-west India, it would be : *Bharatala prawas keru ya.* Furthermore, in southern India, there are four Dravidian languages which are neither written nor spoken like Hindi. Hindi is now the only national

Samsingh is ready for school

This school has proper classrooms

language, with English taking second place. All children in India are taught in their local language in the first stages. Later they study both Hindi and English as well as this.

Now let's see what Hindi looks like. Next to English and Chinese, more people speak Hindi than any other language in the world. There are sixty-one letters in the alphabet. It is a *phonetic* system of writing. This means that words are written exactly as they sound, which is different from English. In English we must learn that *cough* is spelled c-o-u-g-h, rather than k-o-f, which is more the way it sounds; but in Hindi every word is written exactly as it sounds.

81

On this page you can see many of the letters of the Hindi alphabet. It is written from left to right as in English. After the letters of a word are put together, there must be a line on the top, touching the heads of the letters in the word, like this ————————. This line is very important because it shows when a word has been completed. Most of the Indian languages are written in this alphabet, called Devanagari script. All of the languages which use this script have a certain number of words in common.

There is another language, spoken by quite a few Indians, which uses Persian letters. This language is called Urdu. It is also the most important language of Pakistan. Urdu is written from right to left.

क ख ग घ ङ

च छ ज झ ञ

ट ठ ड ढ ण

त थ द ध न

ौ –औरत कौवा

ˮ –अंगूर उँट आँख

Indian children
at a mission
school

Many Indians speak Bengali, the main language of Bangladesh. This means that the people of Bangladesh can talk to their Indian neighbours but not to the Urdu-speaking people of Pakistan who were once their compatriots in the divided Pakistan. Often educated Indians must speak English in order to understand each other.

From what we have read, it seems that Indian boys and girls live hard lives. Most people are poor; their homes are small; many boys and girls cannot go to school. Outsiders who visit India are always impressed with the poverty. This is especially so in the big cities, where many people have nowhere to sleep except on the pavements. At the big railway station in Calcutta, there are families who have lived on the station platform for months. In the cities, there are many beggars. And all over India, there are holy men, or religious

83

beggars, who are fed by believers. There are about three million of these holy men who live by begging. However, as we have said, India is a land of great contrasts. There are some extremely wealthy people who live in homes which are like palaces. There are many modern-minded families who no longer follow ancient Hindu ways. And even among the poor, there is fun. Let's learn about some of the big festivals of India and of some of the things which Indian boys and girls do for fun.

There are many, many festivals connected with the Hindu religion. Holi is the festival celebrating the coming of spring; the festival of Dussehra comes at the end of the rains. Divali, or the festival of lights, comes at the beginning of winter. During this festival, houses and whole cities are bright with hundreds of lights. There are also fireworks and feasts. Boys and girls like Divali because during this festival there are three weeks of school holidays.

Then there are especially holy places which devout people like to visit. Every year thousands of people go to bathe in the waters of the Ganges, which is India's most holy river. Hindus believe in ritual purification through bathing in a sacred river. The Ganges is called "Mother Ganges", and towns along its banks are visited by tens of thousands of people.

There are many holy places along the Ganges, but the city of Benares is the most important. When Hindus die, they are cremated. Just as it is the wish of all good Moslems to visit Mecca, the Moslem holy city, it is the wish of Hindus that their ashes may be scattered on the Ganges at Hardwar. If you were to visit Hardwar, you might think that there was a great fire; for everywhere along the river bank, smoke rises from the burning *ghats*. These are stone steps on which the bodies of the dead are placed for cremation. A pilgrimage to Benares or to some other Hindu holy place is serious business for the grown-ups. For the children, however, these trips are exciting and interesting.

On this page, there is a picture which shows another form of fun which Indian boys and girls love. The oxcart is advertising an American film! However, Indians do not have to rely on American or other imported films. India has its own film industry—a very big one which makes more films than any other country in the world.

Planting rice in eastern India

Farmers and Factories

About 70 per cent of India's people are farmers, for India is predominantly an agricultural country. Indian farmers must raise the rice that is the most important food in southern and eastern India, and the wheat that is important in the north. India is the second largest producer of rice in the world.

We might be surprised at some of the other important crops. India is third in the world as a grower of tobacco. India produces more peanuts and tea than any other nation. If your mother has ever given you a dose of castor oil, you probably can thank India; for it is one of the world's leading producers of the castor bean. India is also a leading producer of jute, a plant which is grown on the damper areas. Its fibre is used for making canvas, sacking and matting.

Cotton is another important product; the making of cotton and other cloth is India's most important industry. Steel,

86

machinery, chemicals, rubber goods and cars are also made in large quantities. At the end of the Second World War, India was among the ten biggest industrial countries of the world. Its forested areas produce fine timber, including teak, a very hard wood. Beneath the ground, there are rich deposits of iron ore, coal, manganese, and mica.

A good transportation system is important for farmers and factories alike. India is fortunate in that the British built an excellent system of roads and railways. Since becoming independent, India has added more roads. It is interesting to notice that India is among the few countries in the world where all mail going any long distance is carried by air at no extra cost. The Indians call this the All-Up Programme. This means that all the mail goes up—by air.

India has excellent air passenger services within the country and also to other parts of the world. The planes of Air-India International fly to Europe, Africa and most of the capital cities of the Far East.

With its planes, trains, and thousands of buses, India also

Indian farmers are eager to try out new equipment like this tractor

has other less modern ways of travel. Oxcarts and camel carts are common. In many small towns the *tonga* is also used. This is a two-wheeled horse carriage in which the passengers face the rear.

All over India, we see varieties of the rickshaw, or jin-rickshaw. Rickshaws were first used in Japan, and for many years were pulled by a man who ran between two long shafts. There are no longer any rickshaws in Japan, and in other parts of Asia, the rickshaw has been changed to become a pedicab. In this, a bicycle is fastened between the shafts so that instead of trotting, the pedicab man pedals. Old-style rickshaws are still used in Calcutta, Madras and other cities of southern India. Pedicabs have taken their place in Bombay and Delhi. In other cities, three-wheeled motor scooters are now used instead of pedicabs or rickshaws.

Now we will read about India's problems and what she is doing to overcome them.

One of the many buses on India's highways

India's Problems

India's chief problem is poverty. Vast numbers of people have to survive on too little food and live in unsatisfactory dwellings. The result is malnutrition and disease. As numbers keep increasing, the little that there is has to provide for more people. So if nothing were done the people would face eventual famine and destitution.

The effects of poverty are not felt only in the shortage of basic things such as food. On a large scale it means that vital services like schools cannot be set up for lack of money. People are denied the opportunities they need while their strength is sapped through the hardships they have to bear.

Obviously the first thing to do is to face up to this problem. The country must somehow be forced to produce more wealth so that everyone can have all the basic requirements of life. Against India's background of poverty, this is a huge task.

The idea behind producing more wealth is to see that everyone may have what he needs. As we have seen, India is still a country where the very rich and the terribly poor live side by side. Till recently the contrasts in wealth were even greater. Now the country is aiming at a fairer distribution of money among all its people. Even more important than giving each man what he requires is to provide for the people

New skyscraper flats in Bombay

as a whole those things that are necessary for their well-being, including schools, hospitals and roads.

If we ask where this new wealth is to come from, the answer must be from the people themselves and their country. New ways of working have to be learned and the old methods cast off. This is especially true of agriculture. About seventy per cent of Indians work on the land, yet the food they produce is not enough. The same land could give much more if worked differently. People have to be taught and persuaded to give up the methods used by their forefathers for thousands of years and take to better, newer methods. This is the challenge that the Indian nation faces.

While so much of the emphasis must be on agriculture, the people also need equipment like trains, electricity in their

90

homes, a good supply of cloth, and various other things that are taken for granted in richer countries. To meet this need, India has to build a lot of factories, dams and other industrial structures. The country has been very successful in its industrial development. In many places newly-completed projects are helping to create the wealth without which no progress can be made.

One result of the growth of industry has been the lessening of caste distinctions between people. We saw earlier how individuals were separated from each other by the caste system. As one caste often did only one kind of work, it gave its members a chance to live more or less apart from others. But a big factory employs thousands of workers from many different backgrounds. They all have to live and work together, and

A chemical plant under construction. When completed, it will provide work for large numbers of people

gradually the differences in their castes come to count for very little. In this, and many other ways, a new society is developing in India. People are beginning to be free of the attitudes that bound them for centuries.

The main problems of India lie at home. All the things that are still lacking in the lives of the people must be provided before the country can afford to relax. It is for this reason that India has wanted peace throughout the world, for without peace there can be no progress. In her foreign relations India started the idea of non-alignment. This meant that she was not willing to take sides with either party in the big struggles which shake the world. India wanted all disputes to be settled peacefully and she wanted to help in creating friendship between countries. At first this policy was

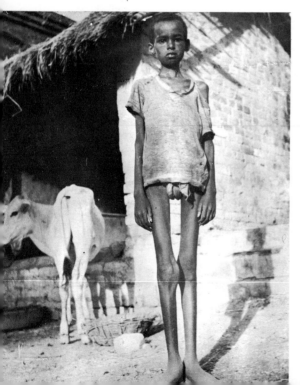

Like this boy, many people in India do not have enough to eat

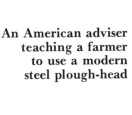

An American adviser
teaching a farmer
to use a modern
steel plough-head

not understood by many. India came in for a lot of abuse. Soon, however, it was realised that India's approach was the only correct one for her, and today non-alignment is practised by most of the countries of Africa and Asia.

India had to pay a price for her policy. She chose not to have a big army and this left her open to an attack by China in 1962. This was a great shock to the Indians who had treated China as a friend. They now have to spend a lot of their precious resources on an army to guard against more attacks.

We have been able to touch on only a few of the problems and dangers that face India, both internal and external. The country has faced them all with imagination and determination. A happier and more settled people must surely emerge as a result of India's present efforts.

Index